Smart Cats

Smart Cats
How to Understand & Train Them

Sigrid & Harald Theilig

Sterling Publishing Co., Inc.   New York

Illustrations

19 color photos from: Photo Agentur Geduldig (1) p. 35 bottom; Ingeborg's Animals (3) p. 17 bottom (Kaufmann), p. 38 top (Heitmann), p. 56 top (Brechbühl); Werner Layer (3) p. 18 bottom, p. 35 top, p. 38 bottom; the authors (4) pp. 36 and 37 top; Reinhard–Tierfoto (8).

43 drawings by: Eva Hohrath (3) pp. 73, 74, 79; Brigitte Zwickel–Noelle (2) pp. 9, 12; Jirina Lockerova (38).

15 vignettes by: Marianne Golte–Bechtel (9), Milada Krautmann (6) pp. 8, 14, 23, 25, 45, 85.

Translated by Elisabeth Reinersmann

Library of Congress Cataloging-in-Publication Data
Theilig, Sigrid.
   [So lernt meine Katze. English]
   Smart cats : how to understand & train them / Sigrid and Harald
Theilig.
     p.   cm.
   Includes index.
   ISBN 0-8069-0538-7
   1. Cats—Training. 2. Cats—Behavior. I. Theilig, Harald.
II. Title.
SF446.6.T4613   1994
636.8'0887—dc20   93-43389
                                                CIP

10 9 8 7 6 5 4 3 2 1

Published 1994 by Sterling Publishing Company, Inc.
387 Park Avenue South, New York, N.Y. 10016
Originally published © 1986, 1992 by
Franckh–Kosmos Verlags–GmbH & Co., Stuttgart, Germany
under the title *So lernt meine Katze*
English translation © 1994 by Sterling Publishing Co., Inc.,
Distributed in Canada by Sterling Publishing
% Canadian Manda Group, P.O. Box 920, Station U
Toronto, Ontario, Canada M8Z 5P9
Distributed in Great Britain and Europe by Cassell PLC
Villiers House, 41/47 Strand, London WC2N 5JE, England
Distributed in Australia by Capricorn Link (Australia) Pty Ltd.
P.O. Box 6651, Baulkam Hills, Business Centre, NSW 2153, Australia
Manufactured in the United States of America

Sterling   ISBN 0-8069-0538-7

Contents

We Want a Cat to Stay a Cat

Our kitten, Paul, was in good form. After galloping out the front door, the little fellow ran into the yard with a flying leap. First he hid behind the hedge. Then, turning suddenly, he climbed the apple tree with lightning speed. Continuing his climb, he carefully tested the more fragile branches until he reached the top of the tree.

In a nearby cherry tree, a blackbird sat, eating cherries. Little Paul wanted to go after it. He tensed his body and, testing the branch beneath him, jumped with full force in the direction of the cherry tree. He almost fell to the ground but managed to grab hold of one of the lower branches. For a moment, the little creature dangled helplessly in the tree, crying loudly. But quickly and courageously, he climbed up again to rest on the sturdy branch.

We had held our breath for a moment, not knowing what to do. We were very tempted to call him back and try to teach him that such an escapade was a "no-no." However, it was clear to us that little Paul was only doing what cats do naturally. The hunting instinct is innate and it took

over when Paul reached the outdoors and spied the bird.

Like it or not, our little kitten is a predator. When the hunting instinct takes over, even *he* has no control over what he is doing, let alone his being influenced by humans.

Without a doubt, harsh words on our part would have been totally misunderstood by him, and his behavior would not have changed to our liking. On the contrary, he would have been insulted and would have avoided coming to us in the future. Not being able to understand our reaction to what he did, he would have been left with a deep-seated mistrust of us.

Cats must follow their natural instincts. If we don't like the way they do this, we must offer them other possibilities. If we try to suppress the hunting instinct, it will come out in other ways. We should always remember that instincts are innate, and if we want to change them, we must do so very gently.

We have very little control over the behavior of our cat. This is just as true for annoying behavior as it is for agreeable behavior. Constant carping

Character

will only lead to the cat trying to avoid us. If we praise the cat's positive behavior, he will accept criticism much better and respect us as well.

Cats have their own life-style. If we show them that we are annoyed at what they do naturally, they will feel restricted and will avoid us. We can even become the enemy. If, however, we learn to see the positive side of their way of life, thereby accepting them for what they are, we will have earned their trust and be better able to mould their behavior.

Cats need a certain amount of freedom. If we allow them some freedom to act naturally, we can both enjoy their agility and cleverness and avoid feeling guilty that we have interfered too much with nature. This has nothing to do with the fact that we want to, even have to, train our little kitten. Our motto is: train, but do not interfere with a cat's innate nature.

The successful training of a cat depends to a large degree on our own attitude and approach to the animal. Remember that cat owners who really love their animals, rather than just love "having them," are much more successful. This means that a cat must not only be given food, water, and shelter, but also care and a loving home, a combination that will make them trusting, confident, and alert.

With all of this taken into consideration, success is almost assured, and you will have a pet that is also your friend.

The only way to have a friend is to be one.
—Ralph Waldo Emerson

The Personality of the Cat

The kitchen smelled heavenly. Peter was sitting on the windowsill, looking in the direction of the stove with great anticipation. His mistress tried to coax him. "Here, Peter, come." Peter approached carefully, keeping a safe distance while licking his lips with his little pink tongue. "Here, kitty-kitty," his mistress called, taking a couple of steps towards him. With a quick jump, the cat took off. She stood there with a piece of roast, but could not entice him to her.

Peter kept out of her way, regard-

less of where she was. He would not allow her to come within five steps of him. His mistress could not understand what was happening. Peter had always been trusting and sociable. What was the matter all of a sudden? What did she do wrong?

Cats Are Sensitive

The more Peter's mistress thought about it, the more clearly she remembered an event that had taken place some weeks ago. She had caught Peter trying to sharpen his claws on the kitchen cabinet. Angry about the damage he was doing, her quick reaction was to give him a few good swats and scold him loudly. In response, he hissed, took a few swipes at her with his paw, and disappeared. He was gone for two days and, since then, he kept his distance.

That's a cat for you! But what to do now? Cats do not take kindly to being hit, to harsh words, or to hectic, sudden movements. Cats don't easily forget negative experiences, and they remain distrustful—distant, cautious and shy—for a long time afterwards. They are guided by feelings that you can't categorize as right or wrong. Often these feelings are the cat's—or our own—undoing.

Just as we often don't understand the behavior of our cat, the same holds true for the cat, who does not understand the reactions of his mistress. A moment ago, she was his friend. Now, she is frantic and loud. Is it any surprise that this small creature can't make sense out of it all? Every now and then, we should think about the part we play in a cat's behavior. In our example, all Peter's mistress would have had to do was to provide a scratching post in the house so that Peter could have used that instead of the kitchen cabinet.

Cats Are Curious

Cats rely on their sense of smell. This is apparent when a stranger comes into the house. First the cat will sniff from a distance and only then move slowly closer and carefully examine the shoes of the stranger. If the stranger seems not quite trustworthy, the cat will walk away.

A strange cat is approached just as cautiously. First the cats sniff around each other's noses, then along the sides, and lastly they inspect each other's tail ends. When a meeting takes place on a cat's own territory, it will display a lot of courage. A cat is prepared to defend its own territory un-

der all circumstances. Generally, an intruder is quickly chased off with much hissing and a few swipes of a paw. Sometimes, however, a cat will tolerate an intruder, and the two cats will patiently check each other out.

Courageous or Fearful?

The larger a cat's territory is, the more courageous and powerful it feels. Indeed, the size of the territory is an important indication of how much

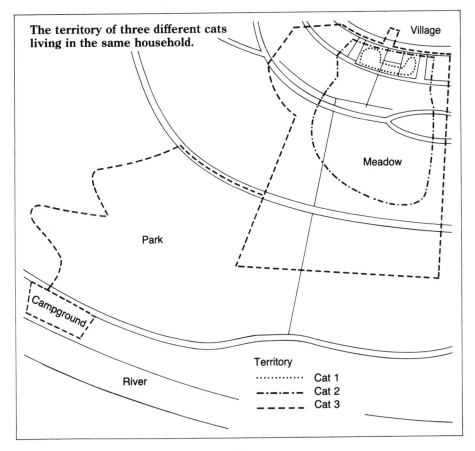

The territory of three different cats living in the same household.

Village

Meadow

Park

Campground

River

Territory

········· Cat 1

—·—·—·— Cat 2

— — — — Cat 3

confidence a cat has.

We had a cat who, even after half a year, was still totally impoverished. Her territory consisted of our house, her sleeping place, and our neighbor's barn. Another cat who came to us at the same time took only one week to establish a good-size territory which she proceeded to expand considerably on her own.

But neither of those cats could keep pace with the cat who had lived with us before the other two arrived. She had a huge territory, and every summer she went on a journey that would have frightened any other cat. As soon as summer arrived, she left to live for six to eight weeks at a campground some distance from our house.

A Cat's Senses

In order to maneuver successfully in a large territory, a cat has to have well-developed senses. (Fortunately, most cats do.) A cat can remember and re-trace the exact route it took some time ago.

Cats have excellent vision and are able to detect the most minute movements. At night, when their pupils are wide open, the reflective background of their eyes detects even the smallest ray of light. We all have seen the eyes of a cat glowing in the dark. In daylight, the pupils narrow to protect against the brightness.

The cat's tactile senses are also well developed. At the base of the five or six long whiskers, there are a number of tactile nerves. These allow the cat to detect anything that the whiskers touch. In tight, unfamiliar places, the cat also uses his whiskers as a ruler. The whiskers are positioned differently, depending on what the cat is doing at any given time. If the cat is resting, they are horizontal and close together. When a cat is carrying a mouse, the whiskers are wrapped around it, detecting the slightest movement. If a cat raises its head to sniff, licks its lips, or assumes an offensive position, the whiskers are bent back close to the cheeks in a wide V shape.

A cat's fur is also very sensitive. Even during sleep, the cat can feel the slightest movement of air.

When a cat pricks up its ears, it's a sign that something is going on. A cat can hear sounds from a great distance away. In addition, a cat can identify the direction the sound came from. Although our cat might be some distance away and out of sight, when we call him he comes galloping to us with his tail held straight up in the air.

How funny cats can look when they have gotten a whiff of something or

are sniffing around somewhere! Some people believe that cats can only smell food from a short distance away. We have noticed, however, that they know exactly when their food is served even when they're nowhere around. Their keen sense of smell allows them not only to find familiar paths and locations but to explore unknown territory as well. Away from home, they studiously read the *Cat News,* that is, smell the markers left by other cats, alerting them that a territory has already been claimed.

For Her, He Will Risk All!

A scent marker is also a signal for the tomcat that a female cat is in heat. Tomcats are very special cats. They will risk their life for their "beloved." Their longing sometimes makes them travel over long distances, and many a tom has wandered away never to find his way home again. Toms will fight for their mate, showing much courage, persistence, and patience.

The way a cat holds its whiskers when: top row, relaxed; middle row, walking and hunting; bottom row, in defensive posture, sniffing, biting, licking its lips after a meal, and rubbing its head against you wanting to be stroked.

Fierce, serious fights take place among competing toms. These usually occur at night and are announced by much howling. The two cats will face each other without moving and stare, making a sound that goes from a high-pitched meowing to howling and growling. Suddenly, they jump at each other. For a moment, the only thing you can see is a ball of fur, rolling on the ground, screaming incessantly. Then they separate and again stare at each other. This contest often goes on for days, until one of the cats admits defeat and leaves.

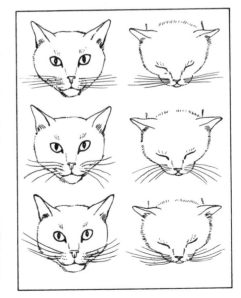

11

Exploring Is Serious Business

Whenever a cat finds itself in new surroundings, it needs to know *where* it is and that there is nothing dangerous lurking about. Only then will a cat be able to trust its new environment.

The way a cat examines a room: the arrows show the direction of its movements; the dots, the places where the animal stopped; and the broken line, the path the cat took to finally settle high on a shelf for a good vantage point.

This is particularly true when it is surrounded by strangers.

We had a chance to observe this when little Paul first came to us. Cautiously, he looked into the room and sniffed along the frame of the door. After taking a few small steps he surveyed the whole room without moving a muscle. Then he went straight to the corner closest to him and briefly examined the long bookcase against the wall. Without hesitation, he ran over to the shelves and busily examined the contents with his nose and whiskers. All cats explore any new environment in a similar thorough fashion.

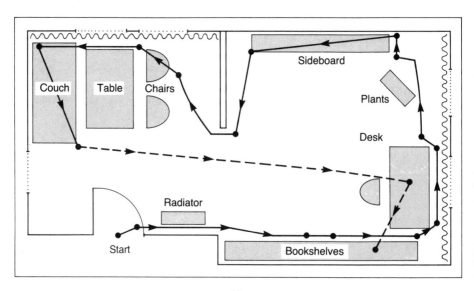

Character

The Cat's Temperament

If a cat likes you, it will often do very funny things: pretend to stalk you, play with your shoelaces, or jump up on your lap, cuddling and kneading you and curling up into a little ball. Some people literally attract cats, and cats have been known to become very attached to people. However, even if a close friendship develops over time, it by no means implies that the person can "rule" over that cat. Cats are much too close to "nature" for that to happen.

If cats don't want to do something, you can stand on your head, and they still won't give in. Inevitably, they prove to be much more persistent than we are.

Specific behavior, of course, depends on the temperament of the cat. Allow us to introduce you to some of the temperaments that we have encountered over the years.

The connoisseur has a lot of endurance, takes his time, eats slowly, and sleeps a lot. He only learns what suits him and what appears to be fun. He seems to be somewhat lazy.

The dynamo is terribly busy. He doesn't have much patience, can hardly wait for his food, and often dumps his bowl while eating. For him, everything has to happen quickly. He often gives the impression that he is missing something. As soon as he is finished eating, off he goes to his next activity.

The lover constantly brushes against your legs, meows every chance he gets, and never misses a chance to cuddle. He comes as soon as he is called and constantly expects to be stroked.

The maneuverer is smart. He cuddles with the expectation that he will get a reward afterwards. If he doesn't get anything, he will quietly disappear, only to come back in a hurry if he hears the sound of the can opener. He is an excellent judge of people.

The people cat always tries to please. He behaves, comes when called, and learns what we teach him. He can also have some of the other characteristics. We won't have any problem getting to know him and to love him.

In the final analysis, when handled and taught properly, every cat loves people.

The Cat as Teacher

Raising the young is another story altogether. Kittens are loved and well cared for. Their mother cleans,

nurses, and loves them. Of course, the kittens are also well protected. Any intruder who dares to come too close is hissed at and (with unmistakable swipes of the paw) told to get lost.

Cat mothers are loving but strict. Any kitten that tries to become independent too soon is immediately hauled back into the basket. If a kitten does not behave, its mother will growl angrily. When a kitten has been really bad, she'll apply a swift swat with a paw. Rest periods are strictly regulated, as are feeding and cleaning. Kittens are taught cleanliness early on. The mother will clean them diligently and without hesitation. Her rough tongue licks each face and goes on to groom the rest of each kitten's body.

As kittens grow older, they become more alert. They climb all over their mother, playing with her tail, and often bite her ears or fur when they are really full of themselves.

The mother's task becomes more strenuous as her kittens grow up. Eventually, she will have had enough and won't spend any more time with them. At the same time, the kittens are less likely to tolerate each other. What used to be plain fun often turns into fighting. The strongest of the litter becomes dominant and makes life miserable for the others. The family starts to separate. This usually happens anywhere between the sixth and eighth week. Kittens growing up outside will roam about freely around the fifth or sixth week.

The Intelligence of Cats

Minka took one peek in through the living room window and left. She wanted nothing to do with what was going on inside. On the other hand, Liesel, who was also looking through the window, surveyed the goings-on in the living room with interest. We were cleaning the cat carrier. For extra measure, we put a soft cloth on the

bottom. My husband opened the front door, and Liesel joyfully jumped through it. She greeted us with her tail straight up in the air. We both were delighted to see her. We picked her up, accompanied by much friendly talk, and put her in the carrier. *That* Liesel did not expect. But by the time she realized what was happening, the

14

Intelligence

door of the carrier was closed and Liesel was ready for the long journey to the kennel. My husband called our other cat, Minka, but she was nowhere to be seen.

"She literally seems to smell when we are going away," my husband said angrily.

Did Minka indeed "smell us out" or did she simply know what was going to happen? Liesel, on the other hand, always fell for it.

Different cats have varying degrees of intelligence. Some cats are able to anticipate events in advance. Others only know when things are already in progress. And then there are a few, like Liesel, who are totally unaware of what is happening until it is too late.

Intelligent cats know from your tone of voice, facial expressions, and gestures what kind of mood you are in at any given time. Often, less intelligent cats also know what you want and how you feel, but they pretend not to.

Let's admit it—intelligent cats can provide some rather exciting moments, leaving their human friends to scratch their heads in puzzlement. Cats know exactly who favors them, and do they take advantage of it! We know of a family where the mistress allows the cat in the bedroom. The master always complains about it and chases the cat out. Whenever the cat hears the master come home, he jumps off the bed and hides under it. As soon as the master leaves, he jumps back on the bed and curls up on the master's pillow. Is that cat intelligent, or is that cat intelligent!

When people are not clear about what is permitted, the goings-on in the house can become quite lively. The longer the debate about what is allowed and what is not continues, the more successful the cat is in taking advantage of what it likes. The behavior resembles that of a disobedient child. In the case of the above-mentioned family, the cat knew what kind of food the master usually served up, his least favorite. So, when the master called, the kitten came. But after one sniff at the feeding dish, with unmistakable disdain the cat would turn away. He then took a position at the front door and waited until the mistress came home. As soon as she opened the door the cat would start to cozy up to her, brushing against her legs, meowing, running to the feeding dish, and coming back to her again. This game was played out until the mistress finally became aware that the poor cat didn't like his food. And, of course, something much better replaced it, since he was such a cute, cuddly fellow.

Intelligent cats are well able to detect family dynamics and take advantage of them. Of course there is the question of what is meant by an "intelligent" cat. In this context, we would like to emphasize the practical side of this subject rather than the scientific side. Thus, a cat is "intelligent" when it can understand daily situations and quickly solve problems resulting from those situations. It should be able to transfer whatever it has learned to new situations. For instance, given a little patience and sensitivity on our part, a cat can be taught to ride in a car, open doors, and know its name.

Giving and Taking

Human beings play special roles in cats' lives. Some people think that cats don't need humans to live a happy life. We don't necessarily agree. Once contact has been made, cats get used to people just as we get used to them. Many examples exist to support our view.

The quality of life that people and their cats share depends on the emotional bond and the affection they have for each other. Obviously, physical contact plays a large part in this. A cat that is drawn to a human being wants to know it is liked. Cats give us their trust and affection, but they want something in return for the friendship they offer. This is their motivation. Initially, human motivation might be different. A person looks at the cuddly creature behaving in such a funny way, brushing its soft fur against the person's legs, and feels a spontaneous urge to pet it. This is the first step towards a friendship.

Real friendship develops quickly when the little creature lives with us under the same roof and petting becomes not merely a ritual but a true expression of our affection for the cat.

This friendship is one side of what

Top: Cats will feel comfortable and free to accept close human interaction only after we have earned their trust.

Bottom: An absolutely perfect place for sleeping.

is meant by giving and taking. The other side involves realizing that cats need their freedom when living with people. It would be horrible for cats to always have to do what we want them to do. They would simply leave, if they were constantly confined. They need the freedom to live their lives as they are meant to. They need to *be* cats.

In return, cats will give people a lot of leeway. They are not very demanding: they don't ask for much. The space that people and animals give each other is very important in developing a true friendship. Both sides should like and respect each other but not "cling."

If we can provide the necessary freedom, cats will love being called. They won't view it as an obligation or a demand. They will understand that they are loved and cared for. Cats will feel respected and understood, and be willing to do what we want them to do. The greatest favor cats can do for us is to respect *our* habits and behavior.

Gaining Trust

Some people believe that cats have every reason to be distrustful. These people forget that animals don't know the difference between good behavior and bad behavior. A cat only acts aggressively when it has been mistreated—deliberately or accidentally.

Actually, cats are very cautious and don't trust just anybody. They never come near some people. They only become friendly when they are sure that they are safe and that people mean well.

If we want to gain the trust of a cat, we first need to ask ourselves if *we* trust the cat. What do we think when a strange cat on the street seems to show affection by brushing against our legs? Very cautiously, we bend down to stroke it; but we are always alert to the fact that at any moment the cat might scratch us or even bite. Also, the creature might be sick or carry parasites. In any case, we have a hard time getting friendly, and only slowly do we gather enough courage to enjoy

Top: When hunting, no tree or ladder is too high.

Bottom: Sharpening claws with relish.

petting the animal. Similar ideas might go through the cat's mind.

When we meet a strange cat, it makes sense to be cautious. But when we deal with our own cat, we don't

Kittens who are bottle-fed develop a particularly close bond to people.

quite understand what is going on. We believe that we have the right to keep a certain distance. We assume that we are allowed to be cautious, but we get mad at the animal when it shows similar caution. Trust between humans and animals means that both can enjoy feeling secure. Both sides need to know that the other does not have hostile intentions.

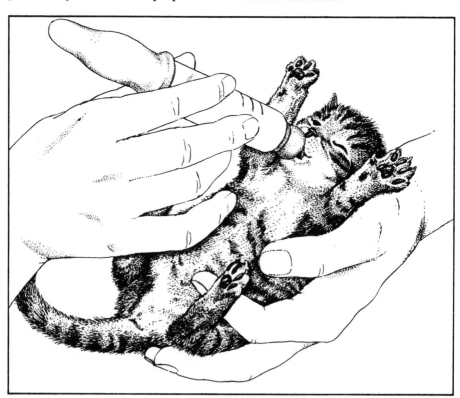

Gaining Trust

Trust can only be established when, from the very beginning, we avoid anything that might create mistrust. In this context, it is important to remember that cats take a little longer to get used to us than we do to get used to them. Many animal lovers forget this. We often hear the lament, "This cat has been with me for a long time and still does not want to come to me when I call." Complaints from cat owners are common. We often expect more affection from our cats than they are willing to give.

Time alone is not enough for a harmonious and trusting relationship to develop. After all, the cat might simply be in the house to have its physical needs met. If necessary, cats can be perfectly satisfied with just being fed, paying no particular attention to the person who feeds them—provided that they don't feel insulted. Subjected to some indignity, the cat will not even deign to accept food from such a person. Obviously, simply sharing a house says nothing about the affection the cat has for us.

The first step in trying to gain a cat's trust is to avoid anything that might scare it.

Do not use food to catch a cat, and do not approach it suddenly. Cats hate sudden movements and loud voices. They also don't appreciate being pulled or pushed away: they flatten their ears and hiss. Don't just summarily pick up a cat, or run after it. They hate that almost as much. If we sneak up behind them in order to catch them, they will pay us back with lots of mistrust.

Trust can only be gained when we proceed systematically and quietly, giving the cats lots of time. Allow your cat to become familiar with the surroundings. It won't relax until it has all the information about a place that it needs to feel fairly secure. This is particularly important when a cat comes to your home for the first time.

Call your cat often and always use its name, accompanied by the typical attention-getting calling sound. But wait to do this until the cat comes to you on its own first. If the cat starts cautiously and first sniffs around you, remain very quiet. Move very slowly. Speak with a slightly raised, but quiet and friendly voice. This is very calming and creates confidence. When your cat comes to you and begins to cuddle, pet its head and sides with the back of your hand. Careful petting is the best way to make non-threatening contact, and a cat recognizes it as affection.

Have a reward handy when petting or when your cat comes when called. Don't forget to offer praise gener-

ously. If the cat hesitates when approaching you, extend your arm towards it. Have a treat in your hand and let the cat have a lick. If the cat withdraws, leave your arm extended for a moment so as not to scare it with a sudden movement. Then withdraw your arm slowly. Extend your arm again, this time with a little bit of food in your hand. Wait until the cat touches your hand all by itself.

As soon as the cat has gotten used to your hand, start stroking it under the chin with your index finger. If it likes that, use the other fingers, too, until the cat tolerates being touched and petted with your whole hand. Always hold your hand out at the cat's head height and approach it from the front. As soon as your cat is comfortable being touched that way, you can also stroke the side of its head and the sides of the body. Then other parts of the body may also be touched.

If you realize that your cat wants to go outside, let it go. This adds to its feeling of being free and unrestrained. Your cat will thank you by coming back home again. This, however, does not apply to cats that are new in your house. They have to remain inside for a while.

Even when you and your cat know each other well and the above steps are not necessary anymore, remain gentle when you approach it. Remember, a cat loses trust very quickly. Some cat owners have had to start all over again with their training after their cat pays a visit to the animal hospital. They have to reestablish the trust they had gained. The training doesn't take quite as long as it did the first time around, provided that the bond between the owner and the cat was good before the event.

Opposite: A cat listens attentively to the words of its "human."

Reward and Punishment

One has to learn how to teach! The basic advice is to be responsible and consistent. Never forget to use lots of affection and love. These principles are important when raising children, and hold true for animals as well. Of course, the difference here is that we are dealing with a different mentality,

Reward and Punishment

way of life, and way of communicating. The training methods themselves, however, are ancient.

Animals respond as well as humans do to a system of rewards and punishments. The mother cat will lick her kitten and purr when it does something well, but she will growl or even threaten with her paw when it behaves badly.

We can do the same thing. Offer a special treat, a kind word, or a gentle pat when your kitten has behaved well. If you are reprimanding, speak in a stern voice. When we train animals, we must consciously try to be very gentle. Nothing should be exaggerated, or the cat may become afraid of us. The cat needs to orient itself to its new surroundings. This orientation is important for proper learning. Your cat must learn what is allowed and what is forbidden in order to avoid problems.

A cat likes to have us acknowledge everything it does right. That makes sense when we realize that we punish much too often. Remember that the cat will change its behavior because of your actions. Rewards and punishments that are used incorrectly result in totally different behavior than we expect. When a cat has behaved well, it must be praised immediately. If praise is withheld until later, the praise will reinforce the behavior shown at that particular moment. The reward of a treat should always be accompanied by calm, kind words and by gentle petting. That way, you won't have to give too many treats. Your cat must first get used to your voice and your behavior. Indeed, talk to your cat frequently and sensibly, just as you would to a human being. A slightly higher then normal tone of voice is calming and instills confidence, while a low voice creates fear and panic. But cats can't tolerate high-pitched or shrill voices. When praising, use just a slightly higher than normal tone that is constant and gentle. When admonishing, use a somewhat controlled, more firm tone of voice, never a shrill one.

As we have already mentioned, we often criticize more than we praise. That is because positive behavior is considered the norm, and we expect it. What is done well needs no special attention. Bad behavior, on the other hand, is immediately noticed. And that can be our cat's dilemma.

We would do well to prevent undesirable behavior in the first place. If the family makes clear its expectations, the cat can better gauge its behavior. All members of the family need to be absolutely clear about what is allowed and what is not. When different members of the family allow dif-

ferent kinds of behavior, the cat becomes confused and, over time, may exhibit peculiar behavior. This usually results in punishment, which could have been avoided.

Being consistent is the best way to deal with insecurities. It is important:
• that the family discuss what the cat is and is not allowed to do;
• that the cat be talked to often and gently;
• that no grudges be held, because

the cat won't understand and will become intimidated (we hold a grudge when we fail to interact with the cat because we are angry);
• that we be consistent even when it is difficult;
• that we always let the cat know that it is loved, even when it has to be reprimanded;
• that we address problems as they appear, with the family working out a strategy for solving them.

"Cat Talk"

Curled up and purring: *I am comfortable, but it is not all that warm."*

Stretched out and purring: *"I feel very comfortable, and it is wonderfully warm."*

For human beings, language is the most important means of communication. It is the way we let each other know our feelings, desires, and moods. Our language is so differentiated it conveys almost everything we want another person to know.

Cat language is simpler and more dependent on emotions. Cats communicate with each other through gestures, movements, facial expressions, and sounds. If we want to handle our cat properly, we should know something about how cats communicate. For that reason we have put together a series of drawings (pages 25–43) and explanatory text dealing with the most important behavior cats display.

In addition to their body language, cats also communicate through various sounds. Although these sounds are difficult to interpret and have not yet been scientifically explored, we would like to share with you some of our observations.

If cats are very afraid, they will tell you so with a deep, hollow-sounding, long-drawn-out *wrau, wrau.*

A greeting sounds like a bright and clipped *rrr.*

When cats ask for something, they use a bright sound, ending with a slightly elevated *mirr.*

If cats are very hungry, they tell

Tail straight up in the air, eyes closed, rubbing against your legs with his head and sides: *"I like to cuddle with you."*

Rolling on the floor, intermittently perking up her ears and looking at you: *"I want to play with you."*

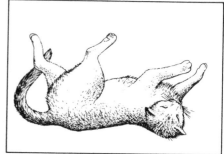

you with a short, loud *meow* that they repeat many times. Sometimes they drag out the sound at the end.

If you do something they don't like, they give a warning with a low hiss that is almost voiceless, sounding something like *chchchch*. This is usually accompanied by a growl that first sounds like a deep *ooor*. It is drawn out and ends in a long, high-pitched *riii*.

Angry cats hiss, finishing with a powerful *khh*.

If your kitten feels comfortable and well cared for, it will purr. The louder and more intense the purr, the more comfortable it is. However, there are some exceptions. Cats who are sick or want help from us will also purr.

The mother calls her kitten with a low, round-sounding *purr, purr*.

Tomcats call their beloved with a long drawn-out *meeoow*, that starts with a growl, is raised, becomes brighter, and ends with a long, deep sound. If the beloved is close by, he will talk to her in a softened *our, our*.

If a cat wants to have peace and quiet while eating and does not want to be bothered, it warns you with a dark, drawn-out, vibrating *our*.

Talk to your cat as if you were having a conversation. Watch its behavior when it makes certain sounds.

Sitting in front of you, tail straight on the floor, looking at you with interest, producing a bright, discreet *mirr*: "What are you doing? Do you have something I might be interested in?"

Approaching you with the tail straight up in the air and a discreet *rrrr*: "Hello. I am glad that you came home."

27

Making Use of the Cat's Play Instinct

By nature, cats are hunters. They have inherited hunting skills from their ancestors. Predatory animals lie in wait, watch, sneak up, and then pounce on their prey. All of these actions are instinctive; a cat can't do anything about them. If we suppress the hunting instinct, the cat will compensate in other ways. Certain key stimuli trigger a cat's hunting instinct. In the absence of such stimuli, or when they are only seldom available, a kitten will react to stimuli that are similar. For instance, in place of the non-existing mouse, your legs could be targeted, especially when they move back and

Galloping along with the tail extended horizontally: *"I've got to hurry and check this out."*

Ears pointing forward, body in a crouch, tail down, watching motionlessly, occasionally taking one or two steps: *"I need to move cautiously."*

Learning While Playing

forth like something in the wild. Instead of a mouse, a cat might also throw a yarn ball in the air or bat it and chase it across the floor.

We call these antics "the play instinct." Very likely, it is a substitute for the hunting instinct. Breeding does not play a part in this. Heredity firmly imprints this instinct in all cats. However, the impulse that triggers the behavior is sometimes more prominently developed in one breed than in others.

What is customarily called "the play instinct" can be more easily understood when we watch young kittens. The hunting instinct is not yet fully developed, and a kitten's play should

not be viewed as a mere substitute for hunting. It is important training for adulthood.

It is dangerous to suppress the play instinct. Cats who have been prevented from engaging in activities that serve as substitutes for hunting often become disturbed. If you have interfered, you should not be surprised when you find that a corner of a room has become the litter box, curtains are being torn, or flowerpots are mysteriously being knocked over.

All instinctive behavior has a specific trigger and a clearly defined goal. For a cat, a mouse trying frantically to run away is such a trigger. The goal of

Front part of the body hunched down, back raised, tail slightly bent: *"Come over here, tomcat. Let's cuddle."*

Arching the back: *"Boy, did I sleep well!"*

29

Learning While Playing

the cat is to catch the mouse as quickly as possible.

We can make use of this playful process during training, guiding individual steps without destroying the instinct. We can choose between training methods, depending on what we want to accomplish. The fact that cats are amazingly intelligent works in our favor. Theirs is a very simple but effective method: they learn by watching. They can do this because of their ability to observe the most minute movements and actions. They are always ready when something new comes along.

If we proceed methodically, using easily recognizable steps, cats will learn just by watching. For instance, cats have been known to learn how to open doors and windows and how to get something out of a closed cupboard. The critical factor in that learning is how successful the exercise is. The more successful the experience, the more motivated the cat becomes to solve a problem. In other words, the more eager the cat will be to learn.

A word of caution: Don't ask too much, or your cat will withdraw and stop learning.

The learning process is always subject to natural law. There are several

Ears pointing forward, sitting quietly, tail on the floor, motionless: *"I have to be really careful, or I won't catch what I am after."*

Turning away and paying no attention to your call: *"I am simply not interested in you at all."*

psychological learning theories that deal with the way animals learn. From these theories, we have selected only those that promise practical results. And with that, let's go back to the real work of teaching.

During play, cats accidentally produce movements and gestures that fit our training concept. If we reward such behavior cleverly, we slowly reach our goal without much effort on our part. This method reinforces existing behavior—the very essence of training. Certain stimuli teach a cat to jump, to stretch, to stand up on its hind legs, to freely maintain contact with us, and to really play.

As we have already mentioned, instinctive behavior is triggered by specific key stimuli. Another method we can use during training is to create artificial stimuli that will show the cat what we want it to learn. Of course, a proper reward is necessary to produce results. Without it, training a cat is impossible. A simple example of what we mean by artificial stimuli and how to use them follows.

Let's say we want to teach our cat how to jump over a hurdle. Place the cat a short distance in front of the hurdle, attach a string to a paper ball, and dangle it a few centimetres away from its face.

Standing with the ears pointing straight up and one paw raised: *"What is happening over there?"*

Body contracted, back arched a little, tail down, ears pointed: *"I must be careful."*

31

Learning While Playing

This artificial stimulus takes the place of a mouse that is trying to escape and triggers "catching" behavior. Draw the string forward in front of the cat and lift it in the air when it reaches the hurdle. The cat will automatically follow and jump in order to catch the "mouse." The paper ball dancing in front of the cat serves as the artificial trigger and, by pulling it forward, you guide the cat into jumping the hurdle.

The cat sees the paper ball as a "mouse." Anything that moves about and is smaller than the cat itself is considered prey. Shape and color are of little consequence. Objects that are close to the size of a mouse are particularly effective triggers. Some cats prefer smaller objects; they are frightened when they are confronted with larger ones.

The direction in which a substitute object moves is of great importance. Objects that move away from the cat in a straight line or that move back and forth before it are particularly stimulating. Circular movements seem to be less intriguing. Objects that move towards the cat create more or less intense defensive reactions. The cat will sometimes stand up on its hind legs or even move backwards.

The cat may also jump sideways with one big leap. Such a movement is

Sitting in front of you with big eyes, licking its lips: *"You have something that I think I would like"* or *"That was good. I would like some more."*

Looking up or down, pointed ears, big eyes: *"This really interests me! Boy, am I curious!"*

Learning While Playing

interpreted as being aggressive. Try to avoid provoking this type of movement during training.

The size of the object does not influence the cat very much, just as it is irrelevant if the cat is familiar with the object or not. It is important to know that a defensive reaction is triggered when the prey changes direction too quickly. From this, we can conclude that the trigger object should only move away in a straight line in front of the cat and that the direction should only be changed very slowly.

In addition to visual triggers, there are also some auditory ones. The most prominent of these are scratch-ing noises. Cats always know where sound is coming from. They look in the direction of the noise, turn their ears straight ahead, remain briefly in that position, and then move to where the sound is coming from. We can take advantage of this reaction, too, as we will see a little later.

Another possibility for training exists when we let the cat get used to a situation from which it cannot escape. In this case we are exerting a certain amount of force, and we must be careful not to overdo it. We need to remember that cats are very sensitive, and they often are fearful of strange objects and situations. Training be-

Flattened ears and a gentle hiss: *"Please leave me alone!"*

Flattened ears and loud hissing: *"Now this is enough! In a minute I am going to hit you!"*

Playing with a mouse is instinctive behavior which we can take advantage of.

training of animals is subject to certain laws of nature. They can best be explained by observing a chain of behavior.

Let's go back to the example of the hurdle-jumping exercise. We have chosen this complex example in order to show you how varied a training plan can be. When you establish your own training program, you can easily orient yourself to the example of this plan. All you have to do is establish the training goal and formulate the individual training steps accordingly.

A cat can learn many things that will make your life together much eas-

comes much more difficult once a cat has been frightened.

We can get cats used to a certain room, to a collar, or to strange surroundings. The individual steps used to achieve this are discussed below.

But first, let's briefly review the principles involved in how cats learn. As we have already mentioned, the

Opposite page, top: By nature, cats are clean animals.

Bottom: Two cats eating their meal in harmony.

Next page, top: A cat playfully jumps a small hurdle.

Bottom left: A peaceful congregation of cats.

Bottom right: A sunny window is a good place to wash.

ier. You can teach your cat to ride in the car, to get used to a particular place for sleeping, to sharpen claws on a scratching post, to come when it is called, to stay away from the flower bed, and other such civilities.

In our example of jumping a hurdle, we used a paper ball to trigger instinctive behavior. We made the cat jump over the hurdle without even realizing it. In other words, this had nothing as yet to do with learning. Learning has taken place only when the cat jumps over the hurdle when you ask it to. For that to happen, we must reward every movement the cat makes while jumping.

How to do this is explained in the diagram. Desired behavior is built one step at a time by using rewards systematically.

Top: Cats are loving, attentive, but strict mothers.

Bottom: If a cat has used the carrier as a resting and hiding place, the first important step in preparing for a trip is already solved without fear and stress.

Stimulus or trigger:
Paper ball moving
away from the cat

↓

Cat's reaction
1. Observes
2. Reaches for the paper ball
3. Jumps after it

↓

Reward
Food and praise when cat
1. Runs after paper ball
2. Follows ball over hurdle

↓

Several repetitions of
previous steps

↓

Cat makes connection
between its reaction
and reward

↓

Cat now jumps over hurdle
when asked to,
without paper ball as trigger

↓

Rewards strengthen behavior
and serve as further motivation

↓

After several repetitions, cat
will jump when asked to,
even without reward

Learning While Playing

Before we take a closer look at the individual steps in the chain of behavior, we would like to say a few words about rewards. It is clear that the rewards must be attractive. In order to increase the cat's desire to come closer to the goal, we need to be sure we're using the appropriate rewards—normal food, favorite food, and special treat.

As soon as the cat becomes attentive and reacts to the stimulus, a small piece of normal food is given. If the cat makes an effort to follow us, we reward it with its favorite food. If the cat really works hard and makes the desired motion, we reward it with a spe-cial treat. It is important to always offer small bits of food and to use lots of praise and stroking.

Training is most successful when we take advantage of other instincts. For instance, cats are particularly active after a prolonged rest period, when they are hungry (just prior to feeding time), and when they need to use the litter box. In addition, scents (the cat's own, that of the prey, or that of food) also play a vital role.

In order to successfully train a cat, you need to follow a few basic rules. These will make the interaction with your cat a positive experience, leading you directly to the goal you have set.

Walking briskly towards a person with the tail raised high, meowing with the mouth open, and looking at you: *"Please give me some of what you are holding in your hand."*

Same behavior and continuously running to the feeding bowl: *"I am hungry. Please give me something to eat."*

Take your time during the training session and stay relaxed.

1. Gain your cat's trust.
2. Introduce all the objects that you want your cat to use (leash, cat carrier, litter box, etc.) and allow the cat enough time to get used to them.
3. Stay calm and do not be anxious when things don't work out the way you had planned.
4. Don't force your cat when sometimes it doesn't cooperate.
5. Don't make sudden movements (even when you are excited because things went well); your cat might misunderstand them.
6. Give your instructions in a calm voice.
7. Do not work with your cat longer than half an hour a day. Single exercises should take no longer than 10–15 minutes.
8. Each individual exercise should not be repeated more than three or four times. Tired cats quickly become impatient.
9. Establish a plan before starting the exercise and think about what meth-

Body tucked in, tail between legs, body close to the ground: *"I am afraid."*

The same drawing, the cat calling *mirau, mirau* **in a low, quavering voice, pressing the upper part of the body to the ground:** *"I am terribly afraid!"*

Front paws stretched out, head and chest lowered, muscles tensed, sometimes accompanied by yawning: *"I've had enough sleep, I need some fresh air"* **or** *"I am bored and feeling a little sluggish. I need a good stretch."*

Learning While Playing

ods to use in order to reach your goal.

10. Don't delay— reward your cat immediately if it did what you asked.

11. Be economical when giving a treat. Always include talking and stroking.

12. When you have reached the training goal, plan to do a few repetitions from time to time.

13. When your cat has successfully learned a lesson, give it a few days of rest before starting to teach the next one.

Following is an example of a training plan showing how you can work with your cat. If you wish, you can reward involuntary behavior, such as a reaction to a noise or maintaining a desired position while being held in place, as well as voluntary ones as long as they also lead to the educational goal. The principle of reward for correct behavior remains the same. It is most important, however, to follow the training plan and build systematically on what is learned.

Clawing a board or a tree with the front paws: *"I am taking care of my claws."*

Body lowered a little to the ground, moving cautiously forward, and looking in the direction from which something bad is expected: *"I think I should walk away from this."*

Training Plan

Training Goal
Jumping over a hurdle.

Intermediate Goal
1. Alert cat, motivate it to move towards the hurdle.
2. Encourage cat to jump over hurdle.
3. Encourage cat to jump over hurdle when asked.

Stimuli to Trigger Instinctive Behavior
1. Make scratching sound.
2. Dangle the paper ball.

Reward (Reinforcement)
1. Praise and stroking.
2. Normal food.
3. Favorite food.
4. Special treat.

Intense hissing, standing on hind paws, hitting with front paws: *"Now I've really had enough! Get out of here!"*

Hind quarters raised, tail down, hair standing up, moving cautiously forward, maybe growling: *"Let me pass"* or *"I have to get away from this dangerous place."*

– Training Plan

Making Use of Other Instincts
1. Particularly active play phase after rest period.
2. Being hungry just prior to feeding.

Training Materials
A beam or carton set 6 inches (15 cm) off the ground (raised as your kitten successfully masters each height) and a paper ball (newspaper, etc.) attached to a string.

Using Rewards
Food, praise, and stroking should always be offered together. Use only *very* small pieces of food.

Training Schedule
Twice daily, eight minutes each session, but never more than four exercises in a row.

Training Duration
Depending on the degree of intelligence and motivation, up to three weeks.

Additional Suggestions
Depending on motivation and intelligence, shorten or lengthen individual exercises. If the cat learns quickly, the suggested times can be shortened. If your cat is anxious, you might want to go more slowly. You are the trainer.

Individual Steps

Days 1–2
1. Get your cat's attention by making scratching noises.
2. As soon as the cat pays attention, dangle the paper ball in front of it.
3. When the cat starts to reach, pull the string slowly with a jerking motion so that the paper ball moves away from the cat.
4. Repeat until the cat follows the paper ball.

Days 3–5
1. Repeat the steps above. When the cat runs to the hurdle, give it a reward.
2. Pull the paper ball over the hurdle. When the cat follows, reward it again.
3. Repeat the steps above and then dangle the paper ball slightly above the hurdle. Praise and reward the cat if it follows.

Days 6–7
1. Repeat all previous steps: dangle paper ball and move it swiftly in the direction of and over the hurdle. Give a special treat, lavishly praise, and stroke, if the cat follows.
2. After a few successful exercises, use your hand instead of paper ball. Hold a little food in your hand, let the

cat sniff at it, and ask it with the typical *pspsps* sound to follow your hand in the direction of the hurdle. In order that the cat may have a good chance to jump, move your hand in an arc over the hurdle. If it makes the jump, praise lavishly, pet, and give your cat a treat.

Days 8–11
Repeat all steps until your cat jumps over the hurdles without any problem.

Days 12–15
1. If the cat continues to jump well, slowly reduce the amount of food and increase the amount of praise and petting.
2. Lure the cat, using only your voice, and praise it when it jumps.
3. Repeat Step 2 until the cat jumps the hurdle whenever you ask it to.
4. Every few days, repeat what the cat has learned, to strengthen its memory.

Walking on the Leash

The subject of leashes for cats is a charged issue among cat lovers. Some think a cat should never be put on a leash; others make exceptions if there is no other way for a cat to be outside.

We are of the opinion that the situation should dictate the choice at a given time. If you live in a city, close to a heavily travelled road, or if you live in the country near the woods, where there are dangers from wild animals with infectious diseases, there is nothing wrong with taking your cat for a walk on a leash.

Of course, you need the proper equipment. Instead of a plain collar, use a harness that straps around the cat's neck and chest. You can buy one in a pet shop. With a harness, the pressure created when the animal pulls on the leash is spread over the whole chest and stomach region. A regular collar, on the other hand, can strangle the cat.

In order to safely lead a cat on walks, a properly fitted harness is important. If it is too loose and moves constantly, your cat will be uncomfort-

able and will try to get out of it. If it is too tight, your cat will feel constrained, lie on its side, and probably refuse to walk. A harness fits properly when you can lift it slightly away from the animal with your little finger.

To put the harness on, remove the leash at the buckle. Hold the harness with the thumbs and index fingers of both hands at the collar. Place the harness over the animal's back, as if it were a blanket, closing the collar around its neck. Take the chest strap, pull it gently down, and close the buckle.

It is advisable to pull the chest strap

Leash with cat chest harness.

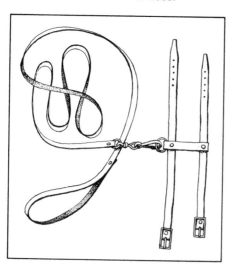

and the collar a little bit further through the loops so that you can buckle them more to the side instead of directly under the chest and neck.

That's how easy it is to attach a chest harness—theoretically! First, however, we need to familiarize the cat with this contraption. That might be easier said than done. If we do this too fast and are thoughtless, we will have achieved exactly the opposite of what we wanted: the cat will hate the harness and hiss as soon as it comes into sight. In order to reach our goal, we must proceed systematically and thoughtfully. The suggested training plan will ensure that nothing can go wrong. Follow the plan step by step; don't be tempted to skip steps.

Training Plan

Training Goal
Walking on a leash.

Intermediate Goal
1. Introduce the leash as a toy.
2. Get cat used to the harness.
3. Give cat the feeling of being on a leash.
4. Teach cat to move with the leash on.
5. Motivate cat to walk properly on the leash.

On the Leash

Stimuli to Trigger Instinctive Behavior
1. Leash introduced as a toy.
2. A moving paper ball.

Reward (Reinforcement)
1. Praise and stroking.
2. Normal food.
3. Favorite food.
4. Special treat.

Making Use of Other Instincts
1. Specially active play phase after rest period.
2. The cat's own scent.
3. Hunger just prior to feeding.

Training Materials
Cat leash with chest harness (never use neck collar only) and a paper ball on a strong string.

Using Rewards
Food, praise, and stroking are always used together. The cat should always be allowed to catch those objects that are used to trigger hunting behavior. This is similar to rewarding oneself. Always use very small pieces of food and plenty of praise and stroking.

Training Schedule
Twice daily, eight minutes for each session, but no more than four exercises in a row. Trying to get the cat used to the leash and harness is not included in this time. You must give your cat time to get used to wearing the harness. Go slowly. Start with 10 minutes and increase the time every day. Once you start using the harness, make sure your walks are not longer than 30 minutes.

Training Duration
Depending on intelligence and motivation, about four to six weeks.

Additional Suggestions
Individual training sessions can be lengthened or shortened depending on the level of motivation; adjust the sessions as you see fit.

Never leave the cat unsupervised with the harness and leash on. When going outside, have a good grip on the leash. Never let go, or the cat could run off, get caught on something, and be in real trouble. Do not go walking outside until the cat is comfortable walking inside with the harness and leash in place.

A retractable leash is useful because your cat can, in a way, reward itself. During training, keep the leash short. Push the release button that allows more length when the cat moves forward and starts to pull slightly on the leash. The leash can be extended fully when the situation allows for it.

On the Leash

Individual Steps

Days 1–2
Put the leash next to the cat's bed or where there are other objects that it plays with.

The first walk with the harness.

Days 3–4
Entice the cat to play with the leash.

Days 5–8
Take the harness apart and put on only the collar. Let cat wear collar first for 10 minutes, then for a couple of hours, but always under supervision.

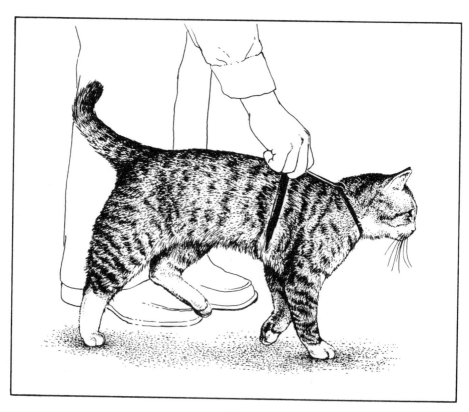

On the Leash

Days 9–12
Add the separate chest strap and proceed as you did with the collar.

Days 13–15
Connect the chest strap and collar using the back strap. Put on the whole

Walking with the harness after the cat has gotten used to it.

harness. Proceed as you did with the collar and separate chest strap.

Days 16–19
Encourage the cat to play awhile with the harness (about eight minutes) and then put on the harness. Stand next to the cat and hold the harness with one hand, pulling it slightly forward and up.

On the Leash

In the other hand, hold a small piece of the cat's favorite food. With lots of praise and with the food held in front of it, encourage the cat to walk forward.

Getting used to the pull of the leash.

Days 20–23
Put the harness on and attach the leash. Keep the leash short, holding it in one hand. With the other hand, take the end of the leash and let it dangle in front of the cat. While the cat is playing, pull on the leash to get the cat used to it. Let the leash dangle farther away from the cat to entice it to walk.

On the Leash

When everything goes as planned, reward the cat with plenty of praise and its favorite food.

Days 24–27

Put on the harness and the leash. Hold the leash at the end. Throw a paper ball with a string attached to it in front of the cat. Throw it far enough so that the cat wants to jump after it. The leash will tighten in the process, and the cat will get used to how this feels. Lots of praise and a morsel of its favorite food should be the reward for a job well done.

Walking on the leash after the cat has gotten used to it.

Days 28–32

Give the cat a sniff of its favorite food, and then put the morsel about 10 feet (3m) away from it. Holding on to the end of the leash, encourage your cat to go get the food. This step is repeated until there are no problems. Don't forget each time to praise and pet your student. Next, walk the cat through the living room without the food as reward, using only lots of praise and stroking.

This step needs to be practised until your cat walks freely on the leash. Continue to praise and stroke after each exercise. Finally, you can venture outside. Your cat will be delighted!

The Litter Box

Cats have always been considered one of the cleanest animals. Indeed, with a few exceptions, cats need very little schooling in cleanliness, because cats won't tolerate messy surroundings.

We have observed time and again that female cats clean themselves more often than males. Mother cats are particularly concerned that their kittens be clean.

It is the mother cat's licking, in fact, that stimulates the release of her kittens' stool and urine. Then, as soon as she has licked their anal region and the kittens have produced urine and stool, everything is immediately eaten by the mother cat. When food begins to replace her milk, she reduces the licking until she finally stops altogether. It is at this point that the kittens' toilet training begins; otherwise, as the kittens grow older, the area surrounding the sleeping basket or site will become very dirty.

Usually this is not a problem since most kittens very quickly copy what their mother does and begin to use the litter box. However, some very young and some older cats must be educated.

The Litter Box

On the other hand, even animals that normally use the litter box will use a corner of a room instead when the litter box is dirty.

The litter box should be made of plastic so that cleaning and disinfecting is easy. Disinfectant sprays are available in every pet store. If the litter box is to be used by small kittens, it should not be higher than 4 inches (10 cm). For older cats, a higher litter box prevents the litter from being tossed over the edge. In addition, the box must be big enough for the cat to use it comfortably. The bottom of the box should be filled with 3–4 inches of litter (about 8–10 cm deep) so that the cat can easily cover up the stool.

If the litter box is in the house, a deodorant spray is very helpful, but the litter box must still be cleaned regularly or your cat might refuse to use it. For a litter box in the house, daily or immediate removal of the stool seems to work best. If the litter box becomes too dirty or is only thoroughly cleaned now and then, you might inadvertently train the cat to be unclean.

If the situation allows, you can also establish a cat toilet outside. If it is constructed properly, your cat can use it year-round. A cat that cannot be trusted outside alone can be walked to the outside litter box on a leash.

Teaching a cat to be clean is a matter of making use of its innate behavior. To do that, however, you must know how a cat uses a litter box.

Outside, cats look for loose ground, such as sand or garden soil. There, they scratch out a small hole using only one paw, changing to the other paw only when the first is tired. Once the hole is ready, they position themselves over it, spreading their hind legs apart, and do their "business." When they're finished, the stool and urine are carefully covered with soil.

If they can still smell it, they will scratch more dirt over it. Sometimes all the scratching uncovers the stool again. If further efforts remain unsuccessful, the cat will finally give up and walk away, even if the smell is still detectable. Obviously, the instinctive behavior of covering up the smell is exhausted after a while. We have seen cats vigorously scratching even a smooth cement floor, trying to cover their "business." When they were not successful, they quickly walked away.

From observation, we assume that cats locate their litter box by smell. In this context, we have noticed that cats will use any place where the smell of stool has been used as a marker when their litter box is not available.

In a case where the cat has used some place other than the litter box,

53

The Litter Box

because it was too full or "dirty," that place must be carefully cleaned. If the outside of the litter box or the area around it has gotten soiled, this too must be disinfected. If this is not done, your cat will use these places when the litter box, for one reason or another, is not available or is unsatisfactory.

When you notice that a young kitten needs to relieve itself, carry it to the litter box immediately. Obviously, this means that you must observe the kitten. Often a kitten will meow, search, and scratch before sitting down to evacuate. If you see your kitten, at the very last moment, spreading its hind legs, lowering its hindquarters, and raising its tail up in the air, you should hurry your kitten to the litter box. Afterwards, the kitten needs to be praised and petted. Food rewards are not necessary.

Cats who need a little longer to get the hang of this should be carefully observed and set in the litter box at the slightest sign that they are ready. After an accident has occurred it is helpful to transfer a bit of the stool to the litter box. Since the smell of stool is a signal for cats, this shows that the litter box is the appropriate place. In addition, cats who are slow learners must be praised and petted more often. Never scold or hit your cat. It is all right to reprimand, but only with the right tone of voice and at the proper time.

Special Suggestions

A cat that never or only occasionally uses the litter box may have a physical defect or been mistreated. The reason may be also simply a lack of cleanliness training. Not being housebroken, in any case, means a serious behavior problem. A kitten should be housebroken by no later than three months of age. Teaching cleanliness after that is difficult.

Problems with housebreaking a cat can be the result of an inherited defect in the cat's senses or brain damage after an accident. In some rare instances, lack of intelligence can interfere with housebreaking. Another possibility may be organic problems in the digestive system or in the urethra.

Top: Fighting for dominance can't be avoided when several cats live in the same house, but usually the fights are harmless.

Bottom: A cat lies motionless in wait for prey—a mouse or a bird, it does not matter.

54

Top: *Attention! Strange dog in sight!* With every hair standing on end and an arched back to look more imposing, the cat stares in the direction of the threat, always ready to take flight, or to fight when necessary.

Bottom: With a little patience and luck, cats and dogs can become the best of friends.

These problems are often observed in older cats.

Psychological problems can also interfere with a cat's routines, including the use of the litter box. These problems can arise from mistreatment or from issues of rivalry. For instance, a cat may leave stool and urine in several corners of the house when, all of a sudden, things that had been allowed are now forbidden. Lapses by previously housebroken animals can also happen when their humans' behavior inexplicably changes and the humans react differently than they have in the past, or when they don't pay attention to the little creature. Another reason is the arrival of a new cat.

By the way, a tomcat that has not been fixed may also soil the house. He is simply being very thorough in marking his territory.

Table Manners

The way to a cat's heart is through its stomach. This becomes obvious whenever we are about to sit down to a quiet meal. How well cats know how to get our attention! They look at us with adoring eyes, prancing around, even trying to jump up on our lap. They act particularly sweet and devoted at our dinner time. Sometimes they even manage to make us feel guilty!

In our house, after a long struggle (as happens with most cat lovers), we decided to put an end to this game. Of course, our cats weren't very happy. They continued to demand their tribute and often used various cat antics to make us give in. Our efforts to reform them remained fruitless for some time, and we were close to giving up teaching table manners. However, we kept thinking about it.

Table Manners

How could we help our little beggars to change? First we searched for what we had done wrong, and we found plenty.

• In the beginning, we treated our cats as if they were people, and we let them get away with too much.

• We liked having the animals around us, and we wanted them to feel comfortable in our home. This reinforced their misbehavior.

• When they pleaded long enough, we

The nibbler.

Table Manners

often fed our cats outside of their normal feeding time.

• After we finished our meals, we often picked the cats up and held them on our lap.

• We sometimes gave them food directly from the table.

• We did not object when the cats made themselves at home on the kitchen chairs or the bench at the kitchen table.

• We kept their food dishes in the

How easy it is to give in when a cat is begging!

Table Manners

kitchen and did not fill them before we sat down to eat.

Then we debated how to use what we had learned and how we could re-educate our cats. Over time, we were able to figure out five simple steps which, after an extended period, worked well for our cats.

Time and again we found that cats react quickly to these simple rules:

1. Whenever a cat jumps on the table, on your lap, or on a chair at mealtime, pick the cat up and, with a firm "No," set it in front of its own food dish. It doesn't matter how close the dish is to the dinner table.

2. Completely eliminate giving the cat food from the table. The cat must eat only from its own food dish.

3. Get your cat used to a certain feeding time. When you sit down to dinner, give the cat its food also. Don't feed it before or after! If fed before, the cat may gulp down its food and see if there isn't something more coming from the table. Anyone who thinks that a cat with a full stomach won't beg is in error. Once a cat learns that begging works, no matter how much it may have eaten it will ask for more and gulp down anything that comes from the table.

4. Whenever a cat is finished with its meal, don't allow it to linger around the table. Pick it up and put it in its basket or another room, or let it go outside.

5. If a cat wants to snuggle up to you and go to sleep while you are at the dinner table, pick it up and put it where it usually sleeps.

All you have to do is be patient and persevere while the cat gets used to the new routine. Just don't be unkind to your little friend. Always be consistent and loving.

Kittens can be trained from the beginning so that later they will "behave like a grown-up cat."

If success does not come as quickly as you think it should, don't despair. Everything takes time.

The Cat's Bed

Most cats are affectionate and like to cuddle. Of course, this is exactly why many cat lovers are so fond of them. It's difficult to withhold a favor when they are obviously begging. So, when the cat follows us into the bedroom, going under the bed or on top of it, we often tolerate it, even if we feel a bit guilty about it.

On the one hand, it's nice to see that the kitten feels so comfortable. On the other hand, we feel an aversion from somewhere deep inside to having an animal in our bedroom.

Our natural apprehension serves a very good purpose: it protects us from possible health problems that can develop when humans and animals share the same places. Many infectious diseases have been transmitted to people in this way. Your cat can never clean itself well enough to be acceptable in your bed. Just imagine that your cat has just come in from outside or from having used the litter box. Now it wants to cuddle up in your bed. In short, no matter how lovable and cute a cat or kitten is, we believe it has no business being in your bed.

In addition, cats need to know where their area is. This is something we, too, need to respect. The area includes the place where the cat sleeps. The sleeping place should be where it is quiet and where the animal feels secure and comfortable. We can easily observe this need for security and comfort. Given a chance, the cat will find something to slip under or a carton in which to hide.

A cat's bed should be enclosed and out of the way, but the cat should be able to see what is going on around it. Because our cats are delighted with their secure places, they are a lot less inclined to come into our bedroom.

It really is not very difficult to teach cats not to lie on beds. You just have to be as persistent, consistent, and patient as the cats themselves are. If they are somewhere where you do not want them to be, pick them up immediately and move them away. Use words, voice tone, expressions, and gestures to tell them that this is not acceptable.

Of course, in the beginning, your cat will turn around and go right back to the place that *it* had chosen, paying little attention to you. But this is ex-

actly the moment when you have to stick with it. Cats are very persistent. You have to be persistent, too. Your cat will only notice your behavior when it is incompatible with its own nature. It will hate what you are doing. You can use that feeling to your advantage.

The more the cat dislikes what you do, the sooner it will give in and stay in its own place, if for no other reason than to be left in peace.

Make sure that your cat has its own, permanent place for sleeping, a place where it knows it won't be bothered. Always bring your cat back to that place when it's time for a nap or when it wants to spend the night anyplace else. Only affectionate persistence will yield results. The basic relationship you have with your cat won't suffer because of these restrictions.

The Cat Knows Its Own Name

It is relatively easy to teach your cat to pay attention to certain calls. It will be guided by a familiar human voice that is connected to positive experiences, such as being fed or petted.

When your cat has learned to recognize that voice, it will react to almost any cue, provided it has been systematically taught. However, you must be patient and allow your cat the time it needs to learn.

As with all training, we never force anything, because cats should have fun while learning. Forcing a cat does not make for a good relationship, and you would never achieve your goals anyway.

Training Plan

Training Goal
Learning to recognize own name.

Recognizes Own Name

Intermediate Goal
1. Create trust.
2. Get cat used to your voice.
3. Create positive connection between voice and experience.
4. Get cat used to its name.

Stimuli to Trigger Instinctive Behavior
1. Auditory stimulus (most commonly *pspsps*).
2. Visual stimulus (quick thumb and finger movements).

Reward (Reinforcement)
1. Praise and petting.
2. Normal food.
3. Favorite food.

Making Use of Other Instincts
Hunger.

Training Material
Food only.

Using Rewards
1. Praise.
2. Petting.
3. Food.

Training Schedule
Daily, before feeding time, but at other times also.

Training Duration
Depending on the cat's intelligence, up to six weeks.

Additional Suggestion
Take your time and don't try to force the cat.

Individual Steps
A time schedule is not necessary since the exercises can be done without a lot of preparation.
1. Read the discussion about gaining trust (page 19) and establishing the necessary foundation.
2. Talk to your cat as much as possible, particularly when it is eating.
3. If the cat comes to you when you talk to it, pet and cuddle it, but only if the cat likes it. Don't grab it or try to catch it when it moves away. It is better to wait.
4. In the beginning, call your cat at feeding time using the typical *pspsps*. Reach out and rub your thumb and index finger together. If the cat comes, reward it immediately with its regular portion of food. Don't forget to praise the cat.
5. As soon as the cat comes when called, add its name to the shortened *pspsps* call. Call the cat in a soft, low, encouraging voice. If it reacts properly, give the cat its food immediately,

while praising and petting.

6. When your cat follows you through this exercise without any problems, eliminate the *pspsps* sound.

7. If the cat reacts when called only by its name, discontinue holding out your hand. It is up to you to decide how long and how much you have to use your hand. Of course, never forget to give a reward. As soon as the cat knows its name and comes when called, give it small bites of its favorite food as reward but don't forget to also praise and stroke it.

8. Reduce the amount of food reward as you go along (here again, take your time) and put more emphasis on praising and stroking. Every now and then, offer the cat a bit of its favorite food, just to keep its good spirits going.

Our Cat Takes a Trip

Travelling is a real experience, one which many cats go through year after year. Trembling, and with sheer terror showing in their eyes, they cower and endure the torture of that sudden long ride. Add to this a new and confusing environment, and the experience becomes too much.

That is precisely what we don't want. As cat owners, it is our responsibility to prepare our cats for unexpected situations so that they survive them without major physical or emotional trauma. Preparing our cat for a trip in a car is one such case.

Preparation begins with a thorough cleaning and disinfecting of the cat carrier to avoid infection. Place the carrier, with the door open, near where your cat usually rests or sleeps. It is important to put a cloth or other soft material that has the cat's own body scent in the carrier. If you don't have such a cloth, put one where the cat normally sleeps. If he won't lie on the cloth or pillow you want to use, place it as close to the cat as possible so that he gets used to it. After the cat has slept on or near the cloth for a couple of days, it will have taken on enough of his scent.

Put the cloth in the carrier and

leave the door open or remove the door altogether. For the next few days, you don't need to do anything. After some initial suspicious glances, the kitten will take possession of the carrier, one step in the right direction. Now it won't be an imposition to be put into the carrier.

As soon as the cat has gotten used to spending time in the carrier, try, in a playful way, to close the door on it. At first, do this only for a very short period of time. Add more time as you go along. After you know the cat is okay with this, leave the door closed for a longer time. Open the door again, and let the cat do whatever it wants. Do not reach into the carrier to pull it out or hold it. The cat should learn that after being confined it will have its freedom again. The cat will remember this and not panic when it has to stay in the carrier for a longer period of time. Every now and then, you can pick up the carrier with the cat inside and walk through the house, putting it back on the floor again when you are finished. In time, the cat will get used to the sensation of being carried, which is uncomfortable if the cat has not gotten accustomed to it. Once you are successful, introduce the cat to the car.

1. Sit in your car with the cat and let it explore the surroundings. Reward the cat with praise and a treat.
2. When the cat is over its fear, get it used to the sound of the motor running. Start the car and calm the cat when it gets anxious. Praise the cat and give it a little treat when it is not fearful.
3. When the cat is used to the sound of the motor, put the cat carrier into the car, put the cat in the carrier, and close the door. Now, drive a few yards back and forth. Do not drive in traffic yet! Afterwards, praise the cat and reward it with some food.
4. If the cat does not show fear, you can drive the car for a short time in traffic. Secure the carrier as described below. After a few more short trips, your cat won't mind being in the moving car. But remember that in spite of the practice and the fact that the cat is used to it all, the experience will still be somewhat stressful.

The carrier can be put on the front seat or the back seat; however, it has to be secured with rope or leather straps so that it will not move if you suddenly have to use the brakes. The best way to secure it is to tie some rope, string, or leather straps to two bottom corners of the carrier. Guide

them back and underneath the seat and then tie them tightly to the other two corners. In some cars, if you want to put the carrier on the backseat, you can pull the strap through the back-rest. Attach the straps to the corners on one side of the carrier, pull them through the backrest, and tie them at the opposite corners. If that is not possible, take out the seat, lay the straps on the bottom, replace the seat, and use the straps to tie first the back corners of the carrier and then the two front corners, pulling the straps tight.

Of course, there are other ways to secure the carrier in your car. Which-ever method you use, make sure that the carrier will remain securely in place if you have to stop suddenly.

Several other preparations have to be made before you and your cat can leave on a trip. Feed your cat small portions of easily digestible food be-fore you leave. Make sure you take enough food, water, and milk with you. Let the cat go to the litter box before you leave. Put a warm blanket that the cat recognizes in the carrier. Take a leash along. Ask your veteri-narian to give you medication for vom-iting and diarrhea—just in case. You may also want to have eye and ear drops on hand.

During the trip, take several breaks. Walk with your cat on the leash. Offer it plenty of liquid to avoid dehydration and other illnesses. A thirsty cat is especially prone to heat-stroke. Don't wait until it is panting to give it a drink. By that time, your cat has already lost trust, and the trip could become very difficult.

We want to caution you not to leave the animal in the car when you stop to go into a restaurant. During the sum-mer, the air in the car gets very hot and sticky and lacks oxygen, creating a situation that can quickly lead to heatstroke. Make sure you have enough fresh air in the car while driv-ing.

During the winter months the car gets very cold, which is just as dan-gerous to an animal trapped inside. Also, when walking your cat in the winter, cover it with a warm blanket or covering so that the cat won't catch cold. Don't walk too long when there is snow on the ground, or when it is really cold. Paws, the tips of the ears and the tail, and the nose can easily become frostbitten. In the wintertime, give your cat liquids that are at room temperature.

Once you arrive at your destina-

tion, give your friend time to explore the new environment. We do not recommend letting the cat go outside by itself immediately. Cats can react unpredictably in strange places. Usually, they try to hide somewhere until they are sure that there is nothing to worry about. In the beginning, take the cat out on the leash so that it can become familiar with the area. Once your cat knows the territory, it can be allowed to go out by itself.

Pay a lot of attention to your cat on the way and once you arrive at your destination. Talk to it and play with it. Your cat will settle down quickly, and everybody will have a good time. If possible, take along some familiar objects, such as the blanket the cat sleeps on at home, or some toys. These will make it easier for your friend to settle down.

The Problem of Claws

Many people believe that a cat is easy to take care of so they frequently overlook the most basic rules of cat care. When these cat owners realize, by the way the cat behaves, that caring for a cat is not all that easy, they become very disappointed.

For instance, sooner or later every cat owner has to face one of the most prevalent "misbehaviors" of a cat: the way it uses its claws. The owner is appalled to find that the new little kitten is climbing curtains, trying to sharpen its claws on the furniture and rugs, or clawing the new linen wallpaper. When that happens, the owner loudly protests and even demands that the claws be removed.

That is wrong. It causes great psychological harm to the cat. Of course, we don't like it when our kittens use their claws in the house. However, we must find ways to stop this behavior without harming the cat in the process.

A cat needs claws to live. This fact

Scratching Claws

is often debated because of the way cats are kept today, but we have plenty of proof. Cats use their claws to remove pests from their fur, to remove dirt from their ears, to fight a rival, to hold food, and to climb trees and obstacles. A cat without claws is only half a cat. We simply have to accept the fact that these velvet paws sometimes turn into dangerous claws.

A cat's paws are a small miracle of nature. When a cat walks or prowls, it does so on its claws. The weight of the body is carried by the five toes in the front and the four in the back. The claws retract into skin folds in the pads. These make it possible for the cat to move around without making a sound. The skin folds prevent the claws from being worn down. A cat only shows its claws when it is necessary to use them.

By the way, a cat's paws tell us when our cat is happy. In addition to purring, its pads will be spread far apart and show just a little tip of its claws (which will constantly move in and out of the skin fold).

It is natural for cats to sharpen their claws. They usually do this when they awaken, after eating, or when they are just feeling good. This is the point at which we must intervene, if we don't want our furniture ruined.

The solution is rather simple: provide a scratching post. If a store-bought one is too expensive, you can make one yourself. A tree branch about 4 inches (10 cm) in diameter and covered with a kind of rope called sisal will do just as well. Just make sure that the rope is tightly wound around the branch. Of course, you can also use an old mat, a piece of carpeting, or a board. The cat does not care very much what it uses.

Put the scratching post or board near the place where your cat sleeps, eats, or spends a lot of time. Now you have to pay attention! If the cat raises itself up and gets ready to scratch the furniture, immediately move it to the post. If you have a board, raise it upright. Move the cat's paws over the post or board, showing it that this is a place where it can sharpen its claws. Cats learn very quickly where they are allowed to scratch. Sometimes it is enough to just show the cat where the scratching post is and what it is for.

If your cat is a slow learner, show it several times. After a couple of exercises, even a clumsy cat will get the hang of it. Praise your cat whenever it

Scratching Claws

finally scratches where you want it to, or at least makes a good effort. The scratching post can also be sprayed with a scent that draws the cat to the post. This is available in many pet stores, but if they don't have it on hand, it can be ordered.

Like our own nails, a cat's claws grow continuously. When they are not used and worn down sufficiently, it is necessary to cut them every now and then. If you don't think you can do it, see your veterinarian.

If you want to cut your cat's nails, here is how: Take one paw in your hand and press lightly on the pads. With a nail clipper, carefully cut only the part of the claw that extends beyond the vein. The vein is clearly visible when you hold the paw up to the light. Always be careful when cutting claws. Be sure not to cut into the vein! Sometimes cats have matted fur be-

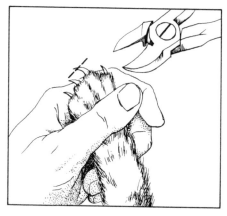

Extreme care must be taken when cutting the claws. Only the very tip is to be clipped.

tween the pads. This can become painful and must also be removed. Keep in mind your cat's personality. Not every cat will stand for this procedure: some will scratch and bite.

No More Stealing

In reality, we can't call it stealing when a cat takes something from the table or a shelf. This behavior is natural. Every animal in the world exhibits it because there is a law of nature that says those who are clever and take what they need have the best chance for survival. Our morals are totally foreign to a cat.

However, among cats, there are certain behaviors that clearly serve to indicate that something is theirs and no other cat may get near it. For instance, if your cat is sitting in front of its food dish and a strange cat approaches, your cat will immediately begin to eat, put its ears back, and growl. If the intruder comes closer, your cat will start hissing, in no uncertain terms telling the other cat to get lost. If necessary, this will be accompanied by a swift swipe with a paw.

Similar behavior can be seen when a house cat happens to come into a stranger's territory. Although a cat will learn after a while what it can't touch when in the stranger's territory, the signals that the resident cat sends are only good for the moment. As soon as the "owner" of the territory leaves, anything goes. The intruder will sniff into every corner and eat any food in the dish. When the resident cat comes back, everything seems peaceful and quiet, as if nothing had ever happened.

On some occasions, we have noticed that the intruder will risk getting pounced on by eating the food in sight of the other cat. This will be done at record speed, before the rival can reach him. After a good pouncing from the resident cat, the intruder usually goes its own way.

Cats who know each other and live in the same house accept a few swipes. They play rough with each other and have some serious fights, but they are friends again soon afterwards. There are many reasons for fighting. Sometimes the fight is about the place where they sleep, sometimes it's about food, and sometimes it's about their toys.

With our cats, we found that eventually they learned to respect their comrades. They stayed away from areas where they were not wanted. This lasted when the other cat was not paying attention and even when

Stealing

the other cat was not present. In the end, every cat had its own place for sleeping, its own food dish, and its own toys. At first, it might seem strange to you that each respects the area of the other. Of course, mistakes will happen, but after a serious lesson has been taught, peace reigns again.

Continuous observation helped us better understand how cats settle problems involving property. First, the misbehaving cat is reprimanded immediately. Second, the intruder is carefully watched so that the resident cat can intervene with a swipe of the paw when the intruder takes too many liberties. Third, the punishment is carried out in a very special way. Under no circumstances is the offending intruder allowed to come close to the place of his misdeeds again.

We have tried to translate this natural cat behavior in order to make use of what we observed.

1. Under no circumstances is a kitten allowed in the place where it has stolen something.
2. The behavior of the animal needs to be watched in order to find out what it is that is so enticing.
3. If the cat is caught in the act, appropriate steps have to be taken.
4. We have to make sure that the cat is not tempted through our own laziness.

If you have worked through the sections above on table manners and sleeping quarters, you are halfway towards solving misbehavior problems.

It is not easy to catch your cat in the act. When you leave the room, your cat will probably be in its usual place. When you return, it will still be there. What happened, if anything, while you were away is shrouded in mystery. Before you initiate any disciplinary action, make very sure that it was Butch who ate the beef. You have to eliminate any possibility that it could have been Boots, or Whiskers, or that all three have shared in the catch. Even then, you can't discipline any of them because you don't know which one of the three was the instigator. Only a very general disciplinary action is appropriate, such as banning all three from the place of the crime.

If there is no doubt that Butch ate the food, take him back to his special place and reprimand him in a firm but not too stern voice. Watch his face. You can tell if he knows what is being said. Usually, he will pull his ears back slightly and tuck in his tail a bit. Don't react too strongly at this point, and under no circumstances should you hit the animal. That will only make him turn away in the future from any movement you make with your hand, and everything you had accomplished

in your training so far would be lost. Your cat will remember a simple reprimand. When you are finished, take the cat out of the room.

For the next several days, keep a close eye on your cat. Check to see if there might be a deficiency in the food he is getting. It is possible that the cat is going after something containing a nutrient that is missing in his food. Animals know what is missing from their diets. They recognize when and where it is available. As the cat's owner, keep that in mind. If you suspect that there is a dietary deficiency, talk to your veterinarian. Make the adjustments, but continue to keep an eye on your friend.

If your cat steals again, reprimand him and banish him from the room. Buy cat repellent and spray it in front of the door and up to about 18 inches (45 cm) on the door frame. (Make sure that you use a spray that isn't harmful to pets or humans and will not damage the floor or the paint on the door frame.) Keep the door closed. After a week, let the cat into the room once more. If he steals again, slap the floor *in front of* his paws with a rolled-up newspaper. (Do not hit the cat directly on the paws or anywhere else on the body with the newspaper. And under no circumstances should you hit the cat with your hand.) The reason for this quick response is to give your cat an unmistakable signal. Afterwards, reprimand him again and remove him from the room.

Some cats will stop misbehaving, but others are less impressed by such behavior-modification techniques. For the latter, it is necessary to remove all food and to keep it where the cat cannot get at it. Of course, this is not always possible. Still, you should be able to expect that your cat won't be stealing food even if he is left by himself for a few minutes. And, with a few lapses now and then, that is an achievable goal.

Don't despair if your efforts are not immediately successful. Simply continue repeating the routine of reprimand, banishment from the room, and newspaper until the cat gives up the behavior.

The Cat and the Flower Bed

Often cat owners are also the proud owners of gardens. They love beautiful flowers as much as they love their animals. It is very frustrating for them when their own or a stray cat starts to scratch in their flower or vegetable garden. Young cats in particular love to play hide-and-seek, and large plants are such a temptation. Flowers that are blowing in the wind seem also to issue an invitation. The cat owner can't be faulted for summarily removing the cat from the garden.

However, real cat lovers don't even let things get to this stage. They protect their flower and vegetable beds while making sure that they are not being unfair to the cat. The measures are relatively simple but very successful.

Of course, there is no guarantee that your garden will be absolutely cat-proof. One kitten or another may get

Cats' playground: All kinds of things that cats enjoy are tied with string to a horizontal pole: a ball of yarn, a toy ball, a crumpled sheet of paper that makes rustling sounds when touched, etc.

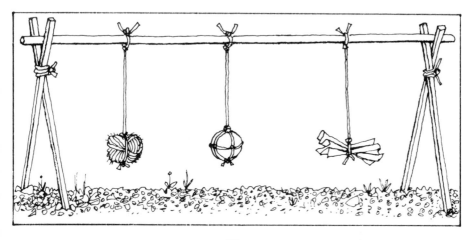

into the flower beds by chance, but certainly your garden won't be used as a playground anymore.

That is important, because the problem is more serious than the destruction of some plants. It is a question of hygiene. Cats who play in the dirt often use the same area as a litter

This device will help keep your cat away from the flower bed. Attach aluminum-covered cardboard to a rope. Suspend the rope between two posts positioned at the edge of the flower bed. The rope needs to be low enough so that the cardboard pieces will move along the cat's back when it tries to walk under it. This is very uncomfortable for cats, and most will consider this device a barrier and will not go beyond it.

box. This can present a health hazard to humans. Cat stool can transmit a number of infectious diseases. (If you have cats and a vegetable garden, make sure that you wash your vegetables very carefully.)

There are ways to keep your cats out of your garden without depriving them of too much freedom. A litter box in the vicinity of the garden can be helpful. You can simply fill a hole with sand. When you notice that the cat needs to use the litter box, take it to the sand-filled hole you made. After the first few times, the cat will get used to this alternative and leave your garden alone.

In addition, you can build a playground for your kitten to keep it out of your garden (see drawing page 73). Now the kitten has its very own place

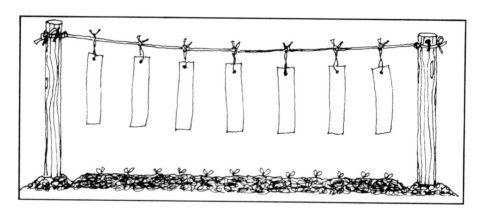

74

that stimulates the play and hunting urge. This simple equipment is much more interesting than some plants moving in the wind. You can even add a few wooden blocks or boards for the kitten to hide behind.

Several cats can play catch together in this area, which they often do with great enthusiasm. The construction that you have built becomes even more inviting when you give it a light spray of catnip. The combination keeps them much longer at their play and stimulates them to get a real workout.

If cats continue to get into your garden, you can build an additional system that will keep them away. It is not very expensive and takes little time (see drawing page 74). The secret of this system is that cats are very cautious about anything that moves just above their head and about things that are taller than they are. The strips that hang down and touch their back are very uncomfortable for them. The combination in this system is enough to make them avoid your flower and vegetable beds altogether.

Of course, it is not necessary to erect everything all at once. Establish a litter box first and see if it is sufficient to keep your cat away from the garden. If it is not, erect the playground and continue your observation. Do everything step by step.

Dogs and Cats

People often talk about the hostility between dogs and cats. If we watch the behavior of both animals when they meet outside, that opinion would be confirmed. The cat raises its fur, tucks in its tail, and scrunches up like an accordion, trying to appear bigger by arching its back. The cat will also hiss furiously. On a leash, the dog races towards the cat, barking like crazy, trying to catch the cat regardless of how difficult it is for its owner to keep up.

The question is, where did this animosity originate, and is the behavior really that of enemies as we under-

Dogs and Cats

stand the term? According to this behavior, the dog's hunting instincts are stimulated by the sight of a smaller, moving animal. This is the same reaction cats have. In addition, the animals don't know each other. Thus, the hunt instinct is set in motion, and it should be taken seriously. This has nothing to do with "being enemies" as we understand the term. The animals don't feel hatred or resentment towards each other; they simply follow their natural instinct to hunt.

However, when a dog is encouraged or even rewarded by its owner, the cat and dog can become real enemies. We know a dachshund who goes wild, running to the door to get to the cat even when his master only imitates the sound of a cat.

However, neither the hunting nor the enmity is necessary. We all know of examples of real friendship between a dog and a cat. The training we give them is the deciding factor in whether dogs and cats live in peace or make war. As responsible animal owners, we should train our house pets to live in peace with each other. This is not doing injustice to their nature because we, and they, live in a civilized society and not in the wild.

Getting cats and dogs used to each other is not very difficult when the an-imals are young. Problems develop when at least one of the two animals is no longer a puppy or kitten. However, these problems can be solved.

When the animals are first introduced, it is important for them to be relatively free of anxieties. This can be accomplished by making use of their sense of smell. Take a cloth and put it where the kitten is sleeping. Put another one where the dog is sleeping. Then exchange the cloths and let the animals sniff at each other's cloth. Hold the cloth in your hand and speak quietly to the animal. Put the cloths back in their respective sleeping places at the side of the animal's head. Continue this routine until you can detect that both animals have become used to the strange scent and perceive it as totally normal.

Now you can bring the two animals together. If possible, do this in a large room. Leave enough distance so they can explore each other. Try to stay out of it as much as you can so as not to add to the existing anxiety. If the animals are already grown up, it is advisable to keep them on leashes.

You should also provide a means for the cat to escape. A bookcase that is high enough to jump on in an emergency is sufficient. Repeat this exercise until the dog and cat accept each

other. Be positive. Always encourage both animals with words of praise. If you have prepared everything carefully and skillfully, you will have no difficulty. You will learn that cats and dogs play with each other, lick each other, and can become excellent friends. In each situation, be cautious and take it slowly so as not to overtax the animals.

Birds and Cats

Now we come to one of the most difficult problems in the training of cats. Unfortunately, there is no real solution to this problem. We shall, however, investigate how we can try to keep cats from catching birds, or how we can at least diminish this unwanted behavior.

Some cats are real bird catchers. Others don't seem to pay much attention to them. It is the hunting and playing instincts that stimulate bird-catching behavior. As far as this instinctive behavior is concerned, the cat doesn't care if it is a mouse or a bird that is moving about. The hopping movements of a bird and the whipping of the tail feathers, however, do represent particularly powerful stimuli to some cats.

Added to this is the fact that nowadays there are fewer and fewer stimuli available to satisfy a cat's hunting and playing instincts. The mouse population has decreased in and around cities, but birds are still found in abundance and cats are lured by them. (Country cats are much better off, but even among them we find real bird specialists.)

Training alone will not be enough to keep most cats from catching birds. The best you can do is to discourage them. Something more is needed. This includes setting rules for behavior (directed more at ourselves than the cat), using technical means, and using chemical substances. Let's begin with familiar training methods. By establishing rules for our behavior, we

Birds and Cats

hope to in turn influence the behavior of the cat.

It is well known that cats like to present us with their catch, and also that they want to be praised for their accomplishment. As far as mice are concerned, this is fine because nobody wants mice in the house.

When the cat brings home a bird, the situation changes dramatically. We recommend that you stay calm and remove the bird from the cat's mouth. The cat must be immediately told that you are not pleased with such a gift, but do not scold. Nothing will be accomplished by scolding. Instead, let the cat know that you want the bird to have its freedom. If the bird is still alive and able to fly, let it fly away in front of the cat. Talk to the cat in a calm but slightly raised voice so that the cat can tell by the tone of your voice what you think about its catching birds. If the bird is dead, take it away from the cat with an appropriate reprimand and dispose of it. Under no circumstances should you let the cat play with the bird. Also, the cat should not be fed immediately after this since the food could be interpreted by the cat as a reward.

From then on, watch your cat and when it shows the slightest sign of going after a bird reprimand the cat, us-

ing a somewhat raised tone of voice. Since your cat does not want to lose favor with you, it will be more careful after you have voiced your displeasure a few times. It is important, during this process, that the cat does not get any kind of attention that it could misinterpret as a reward.

Another way to diminish bird catching is to make use of the way cats act after they have just eaten. Cats with full stomachs are better hunters. They have more patience, to wait out their prey when their stomachs are not growling. You can take advantage of the fact that a hungry cat will readily give up the hunt and go to where it knows food is waiting or is easily available.

Therefore, before you take a walk with your cat, give it just enough food to ease most of its hunger but so that a good bit of appetite still remains. After you come back, give the cat the rest of its rations. The cat will learn that it can expect a good treat after it has been out for a walk. If the cat becomes hungry again during the walk, it will remember the food dish waiting at home and want to return there rather than hunt. A sure meal is a lot better than a bird that has yet to be caught.

The time for outside activity should

Birds and Cats

also be chosen by you. During breeding time, when many small birds are about, take your cat for a walk in the early evening or at dusk. During the daytime, walk the cat on a leash. During other times of the year, it is best to let your cat out after midday and then again in the evening.

Some cats go after birds by climbing a nearby tree. If you think that this activity is getting out of hand, a mechanical device can be constructed that will protect the birds. This is particularly important when birds are nesting in the branches.

Cut a rectangular board in half. Using a sabre saw, make half-round cuts to fit the diameter of the trunk of the tree. Using four screws, attach two strips of wood to one of the halves and fit the cutout to the tree trunk. Position it high enough so that the cat cannot jump to it. Have a helper fit the other half of the board against the first piece, and push hard so that there is a tight fit. Secure the second half to the strips extending from the first half with four more screws. Predrilled holes will make this job much easier.

You can also spray the tree trunk with a deterrent spray, but first make sure that the chemicals in the spray are not harmful to the tree.

How you deal with your cat will have a major impact on how it behaves around birds. For that reason, we have prepared an abbreviated list of rules. If you consistently follow every

Protective device that will keep cats from climbing into trees where birds roost or raise their young.

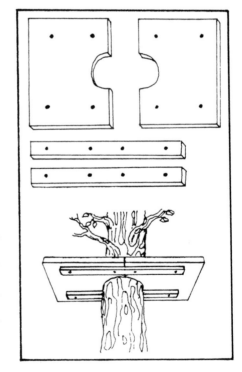

step, your cat will be discouraged from bird hunting. It will not want to lose favor with you.

1. Stay calm. Don't get hysterical when your cat brings home a bird.

2. Talk firmly to your cat as you take the bird away from it, but pet the cat gently.

3. In a calm voice, but with a slightly elevated tone, tell your cat that birds are *not* for catching. Under no circumstances should you scold the cat or chase it away.

4. While your cat is watching, let the bird fly away as you repeat your disapproving words. If the bird is dead, remove it accompanied by the same talk. Under no circumstances is the cat to play with the dead bird.

5. Don't give your cat anything (including food) that could be interpreted as a reward.

6. Observe your cat carefully and admonish it immediately whenever the cat looks as if it is about to catch a bird.

Cats Among Themselves

Dominance plays an important role in the life of a cat. It develops early on, during kittenhood and the young-adult period. During the first two weeks, there seems to be no hierarchical order. Often a kitten will be pushed aside during nursing. The next time around, that kitten will persist because it is hungry. Just as stubborn as its siblings, the kitten will push somebody else away when nursing.

Later, when the kittens become more active, they play their first, clumsy games using the basic elements of hunting, attack, and defense. At this point, a certain hierarchy can be detected among the litter.

The kitten that is the fastest at catching prey, the boldest when attacking, and the bravest in defending will become "leader." It will take a toy away from a sibling and not be seriously challenged. Without eliciting much protest, it will push everybody

Hierarchy

away from the milk dish, and none of its siblings will punish the kitten when it attacks another littermate. We have noticed that it is always the strongest (or one of the strongest) kittens that assumes this highest rank, never a sickly or weak one.

The hierarchical order is not absolute and changes all the time, as if the kittens are simply taking turns being on top. We never saw kittens fight over this issue.

Around the fourth week, when the mother cat brings home the first prey, the hierarchical order becomes more pronounced. The top kitten is now not necessarily the strongest; rather, it is the boldest and most courageous. This kitten will be the first at the prey, will play with it, take it away from timid siblings, and defend it against other siblings. With this kind of bold behavior, it becomes the superior kitten in the litter.

At this point, the order is more stable than before. It remained constant in three of the five litters we have watched, at least until the family dissolved. We gave the leader of one litter to a friend. Immediately, the next kitten in line took over the position. This kitten got hurt when it was four or five months old, and again, without

delay, the next kitten in line became the dominant cat. This change was most obvious when the hurt kitten was playing with a prey. Without protest, the hurt kitten let the newly dominant kitten take the prey away. The new order remained intact even after the hurt kitten had recovered from its injuries.

According to some observers, there are several variations in the hierarchical order among adult cats who live together in close quarters. The variations range all the way from a very strict order to a situation in which none of the cats assumes the dominant position.

We have always noticed a certain hierarchy among our cats. This ranking is particularly obvious whenever a new member is introduced into the community in our house.

Since maintaining peace is a large problem for most cat lovers, we will discuss the systematic way in which a newcomer should be introduced into a preexisting cat community.

The new member must undergo several stages before it is tolerated and then accepted by the other cats. This can only happen when we are supportive but do not interfere with the activities of the resident cats.

The Newcomer

Refusal Stage

When a new cat enters the house and is put down in the vicinity of the other cats, you will observe a clear rejection by the resident cats. They will sit low to the ground with their ears back and their fur raised. With much hissing, they will try to chase the newcomer away. If the newcomer comes too close, it might even get a swat with a paw. The newcomer will not feel welcome and will try to run away. The others will sneak around it. If the resident cats are successful in chasing the newcomer away, its eventual acceptance is not assured.

The resident cats are particularly interested in your reaction. If you indicate that you are not quite sure about the new cat and are, in fact, leaning more towards the side of the residents, the newcomer will be bitterly opposed. If, however, you are obviously on the side of the newcomer, and you reprimand the resident cats for their behavior, you will quickly be faced with a lot of jealousy, from which you too will suffer.

For these reasons, we recommend that you stay neutral. In the beginning, don't get involved in their quarrel. Instead, try the following procedure:

1. Bring your cats into a room where there are several means of escape (bookshelves, tables, etc.)
2. As soon as all the resident cats are together, put the newcomer down (a short distance from the others) and talk to all of them in a calm voice.
3. Sit down in a corner of the room and leave them to themselves. For a time, there will be a lot of hissing and growling. The resident cats will pursue the newcomer, but this seldom leads to an actual physical confrontation as long as you stay neutral. However, if it gets out of hand, you must intervene.
4. The new cat should not be allowed to go outside for the first two to three weeks (this is particularly important for older cats) until thoroughly settled in.
5. Repeat the first three steps daily for one to two hours, until rejection has been replaced by tolerance.

Tolerating Stage

In this stage, the animals stay out of each other's way, maintaining a considerable distance between each other. They will eat by themselves, but is advisable to let them all eat in the same room.

The Newcomer

This stage should last for two to three weeks. Continue to remain neutral, treating all cats equally and interacting with them often. Usually the cats themselves will end this stage and move into the stage of exploration.

Exploration Stage

The cats will move a little closer to each other, and view one another without aggression. This is the time when you can get actively involved.
1. Put the cat down close to the other cats, but stay between them. Now stroke and pet them. In this way, you show sympathy for all of them without the cats coming too close to each other. Practise this for a couple of days.
2. The next step is to move the feeding bowls a little closer together. Feed them their favorite foods. This exercise needs to be repeated until the food bowls are only about an arm's length apart.
3. If the resident cats remain calm, take one cat after the other in your arms. Hold on to each one, and bring the newcomer closer. Let the resident cat sniff the newcomer, and then let the newcomer sniff the resident cat. The cats should not sniff each other

around the face at first. That could be misunderstood. At this point, you only want them to get to know the odor of the other cat. Afterwards, leave them to their own devices.
4. Try to get the cats together often, but allow each cat to go its own way, especially if it pulls away. You can make it easier for the cats to get to know each other by getting them together, serving their food in the same area, and by playing with them. For instance, a paper ball on a string works like magic.

Getting-Together Stage

At this stage, cats will try to play together more and more. Small playful confrontations will take place. You can be helpful by initiating imaginary games which will bring them together. If they get along with each other and tussle every now and then, you can discreetly withdraw. Remember to be equally kind and loving to each animal. This will help strengthen the cat community.

Integration Stage

Finally, your cats will be used to each

The Newcomer

other, will get along, and will have learned to be considerate of the other members. They will accept the hierarchical order and will measure their strength against, and play with, each other. The newcomer is no longer a newcomer. Over time, it will find its place in the hierarchical order. You don't have to intervene anymore. In fact, at this point it is better to let the cats settle any arguments that come up by themselves.

Index

Index

Index